Introducing...
JESUS!

A Newcomer's Guide To Jesus Christ!

Pastor Barry Rudesill

ISBN: 979-8-218-12077-1

Dedicated to "L"

and to all of those who want

to know more about

Jesus.

CONTENTS

Acknowledgments   i

Letter From The Author   2

Reading The Bible   4

1   The Land   9

2   The Baby   17

3   The In-Between   31

4   The Teachings   34

5   The Miracles   44

6   The Passover   58

7   The Death   69

8   The Burial   80

9   The Resurrection   87

10   The Choice   96

Continuing Your Journey   101

ACKNOWLEDGMENTS

I would like to thank Pastor Clint and Mary Lou Rudesill who patiently read draft after draft and offered constructive criticism and input. I would also like to thank my family - Maria, Isaac, and Lauren - who helped me to edit this into a finished product. (I'll take full credit for any errors that remain!) Finally, I'd like to thank all of my campers and students from the last 30 years who have challenged me to figure out who God is and who I am because of Him!

LETTER FROM THE AUTHOR

Dear Reader,

I have to tell you, I never actually intended to write a book. But recently, I've met more and more people of all ages and backgrounds who have never heard the name of God as anything other than a swear word; who have never known that God loves them; and who have never had the chance to be friends with God's Son, Jesus.

Because of that, I wanted to take this time to introduce you to my Friend!

In our modern world, people want to "re-imagine" Jesus. That would be fine...if Jesus was a fictional (fake) character in a book. In that case, you could picture Him as a 50-foot-tall giant, covered in armor, and swinging a flaming sword...if Jesus wasn't real.

But I believe the evidence shows that Jesus *is* real! By the way, notice it's "is", not "was". If Jesus is the Son of God, like we find in the Bible, then He's still alive; He still wants to be friends with us; and He still loves us more than we will ever know!

As you read this book, my goal is to introduce you to Jesus. No frills. No "theology". No big words. I just want to have you meet Him as the Bible describes Him.

In the end, I hope you come to know Him as I know Him!

P.S. If you're ever in the neighborhood, stop by for a cup of tea and we can talk more about my Friend, Jesus!

READING THE BIBLE

When I set out to write this book, I knew that I wanted to include a lot of Bible verses. Don't know what a Bible verse is? Well, that requires a little explanation. If you open a Bible, you'll find that it's split in three main ways:

<u>*Books*</u>
First, there are "books". Most Bibles have what's called an "Index Page" at the start. On that page, you'll see a list of 66 books with names like "Genesis", "Psalms", "Romans", and more.

- Thirty-nine of these books are found in what's called the Old Testament, which involves everything from the time God created the world until a few hundred years ***before*** Jesus arrived.

- The other twenty-seven books are found in what's called the New Testament. The first four of these books – Matthew, Mark, Luke, and John – tell the story of who Jesus is and what He did for us. The rest of these books deal with how the church got started and talk about how we should live if we follow Jesus.

Samples of Hebrew (front) and Greek (back).

These books were written in three languages: Hebrew, Aramaic, and Greek. They were written by around 40 different people; we're not sure of the exact number because some books don't have the author's name on them. Finally, the writers of these books included priests, prophets, kings, fishermen, and shepherds. Oh, and it took over 1,500 years from the time the first book was written to when the last book was finished!

Despite all of this, the 66 books in the Bible tell us the same story: how God, through Jesus, can save us! Pretty amazing, right? Well not really when you consider the fact that God guided all of these people as they wrote their books!

Also, because the Bible is a collection of 66 different books, you don't have to read it in order from beginning to end; you can skip around!

Chapters
Second, there are "chapters". In the Bible you'll find that there are big numbers on different pages. These are "chapter breaks" like we see in modern books. These weren't in the original writings, though; people added them later to make it easier to find what they were looking for!

Verses
Third, there are "verses". In the Bible, you should see a bunch of smaller numbers under each of the chapters. These are verses, and a verse is usually only a sentence of two…or even just a part of a sentence. (Not a clue why they didn't always use full sentences!) Again, these were added later to help people find things easier.

In this book, I refer to a lot of stories in the Bible. If there's any that you want to read on your own, just look for the "reference". For example, if you see "Genesis 2:7", find Genesis in the Index and then go to the page it mentions. Next, look for the big number "2" (that's the chapter) and then find the little number "7" that comes after the "2" (that's the verse).

This is the Bible I use. If you look close, you can see the book title (Luke) at the top, the chapter (the big number "8"), and a bunch of little numbers for the verses. This Bible also has study notes to help you learn as you go!

Now, there's one other thing I need to mention before we begin:

Translations
Because the books of the Bible were written in other languages, they had to be "translated" into English. Because different people translated the same sentence in slightly different ways, the Bible

you use – if you have one – may not match exactly with the one I quote in this book. It should be close, but it won't be word-for-word the same.

Just so you know, some people make a big deal out of this; but, to me, it really doesn't matter. Why? Because, even though they may use some different **words**, pretty much all translations get the **ideas** in the Bible right!

I should also mention that there are some "paraphrase" Bibles, and those can be **very** different! Authors of a paraphrase Bible basically rewrite the words so that it's in simple, easy-to-understand language, and they don't usually try to make it as accurate as they can.

If you want to have a Bible that matches the one I use here, get the New Living Translation (NLT) of the Bible by Tyndale House Publishers. (I like this one because it's easier to read!)

In any case, I encourage you to look up any and all of the Bible verses I put in here! Why? Because I don't want you to take my word for what the Bible says; take God's Word (that's another name for the Bible) for it, instead!

So with that, let me introduce you to my Friend, Jesus...

(1) THE LAND

I was working with a group of Middle School students when one of them asked me, "Who is Jesus?"

Who is Jesus? That's a great question! In fact, it's probably the best question that anyone can ask! Why? Because if Jesus is who He claims to be, then everyone should have the chance to hear about Him and then decide what they want to do with Him!

But to answer this question, we need to take a trip in both time and space! Do me a favor, before you keep reading, blink once. Ready? Go!

Okay, now it may not look like it, but we've just jumped back over 2,000 years into the past! (Here's where I encourage my students to use their imaginations.)

We are now standing in a time before electricity, books, and indoor toilets! At this point, the most common way of moving around is by walking; the only style of music is "live"; and the closest they came to "social media" is actually going into town to talk with people!

But we haven't just moved in time; we've also moved in space, too!

You are now in a small country called "Israel", along the eastern side of the Mediterranean Sea. Israel is about 290 miles long (north-to-south) and about 85 miles wide (east-to-west) at its widest point. If you want something to compare it to, that's close to the same size as the State of New Jersey in the United States!

At this time, the total population in this small country is only around 500,000–600,000 people. To understand how big that is, in 2020, the city of Tucson, Arizona, had a population of 542,000 people. In other words, in 2020, one *city* in America had about the same number of people living in it as the entire *nation* of Israel did 2,000 years ago!

The capital of Israel is a town called "Jerusalem", and there are only around 55,000 people living within its walls. (Where I come from, that's not a very big place!)

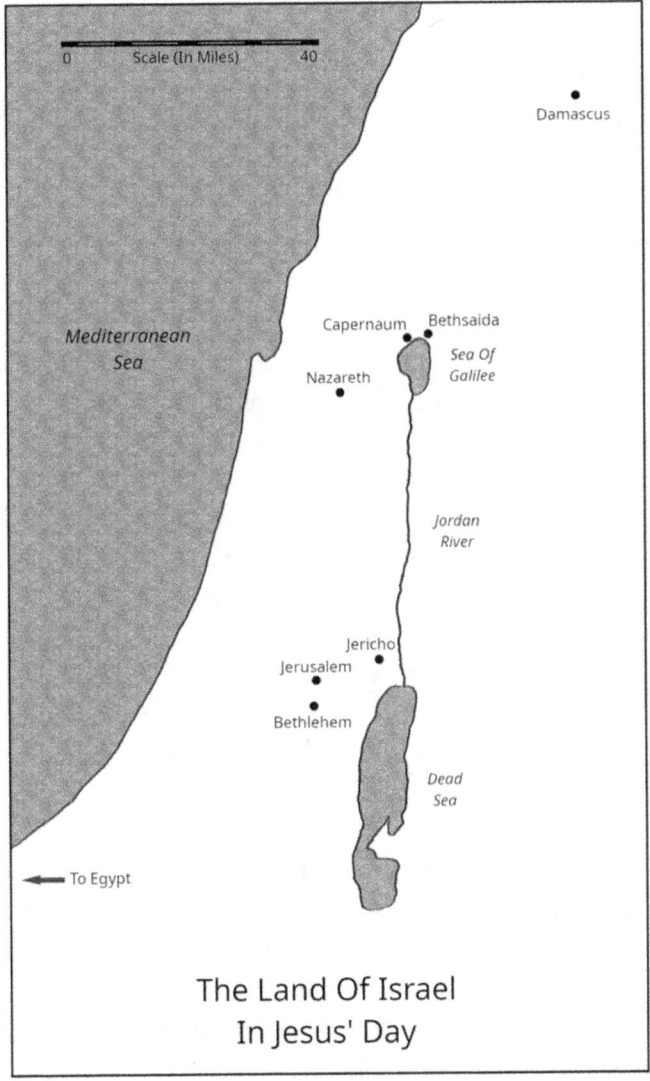

The Land Of Israel
In Jesus' Day

But even though it was usually a smaller town, during special festivals – big celebrations – the city of Jerusalem could grow to over 180,000 people!

Other than the size of the country, you should probably know something about what it was like living there.

Israel is a land of opposites! You can find beautiful farmland as well as a salt-covered sea! You can find mountains nearly 4,000 feet high and valleys that are 1,300 feet below sea level! You can find gardens and deserts, hot places and cold places, wet places and dry places!

As for seasons, there are two main ones: cool and rainy in the Winter (October – April); and dry and hot in the Summer (May – September). In some of the hottest areas, like the Negev Desert, it can get up to 114 degrees Fahrenheit in August! On the other end of the thermometer, the hill countries in Galilee can get snow in winter!

In this land, they had a king. Not a nice king, like you sometimes hear about in fairy tales and movies. Instead, this man, King Herod, was cruel. To get his throne, to become king, Herod killed a lot of people...some of them were even his own children! To keep his throne, he will kill many more!

But Herod isn't really running the country...

You see, if we had gone back about 60 more years, we would have found that a Roman general named Pompey had conquered Israel. (Time travel is tough, so we didn't go back that far!)

When Pompey won, he split the country into a bunch of smaller areas and Rome began to rule Israel. Over time, to make things seem more fair, they named Herod as the king. However, Herod only ruled because Rome allowed him to; instead, it was the Roman Empire who controlled Israel!

Despite the question of who was in charge, life in Israel was pretty...normal.

As a child, there were a lot of different sports and games; some that we still play today! Running races was a popular pastime, children learned archery (bows and arrows), and they had ball games, as well. For toys, you would have had whistles, rattles, dolls, hoops, tops, and even board games.

As part of your education, you would have learned Aramaic, which was the language spoken in Israel. If time allowed, you might have also learned another language called Hebrew, which was the language that the religious leaders used. You might have even learned Greek, which was the language spoken throughout the Roman Empire!

When you were older, the girls would have joined their mothers in learning how to take care of the home; while the boys would have joined their fathers in learning a trade (another name for a job). From that time on, all children would have had to help take care of the family.

Also, at this time, parents taught their children about God.

God? Who is God? Well, God is worth writing a whole other book about! For now, what you need to know is that, according to the Bible, God created the entire universe! He simply spoke and the world was made! Because He's so important, many people – myself included – always capitalize both His name and any pronouns that refer to Him!

And yet God, this incredible, creative, powerful Person did something very cool! In the Bible, in the first book called "Genesis", we find this:

Then the LORD God formed the man from the dust of the ground. He breathed the breath of life into the man's nostrils, and the man became a living person. - Genesis 2:7 (NLT)

Even though God is all-powerful and can do anything He wants, He got His hands dirty when He chose to make…us. That's how much God loves us!

Well, in the first half of the Bible, we find that even though God loves us…we humans didn't feel the same way about Him. We chose to walk away from God, to disobey Him, and to do what the Bible calls "sin".

Sin is anything we do that God tells us NOT to do! God tells us not to lie. Have you ever told a lie? I know I have! God tells us to honor our parents, and to treat them with respect. Have you ever been rude to your parents? I know I have! And the list goes on from there: stealing, hurting others, and even murder!

And, do you want to know what all of these actions have in common? They're all times when we stop listening to God and decide to do things our own way.

God tells us that because we've sinned, because we've walked away from Him, we can't have a relationship with Him. How could we? He's perfect, He never makes mistakes.

15

And we humans? Well, take a look at the world around us. Think about the hurt and the pain we do to each other. Some of you know exactly what it's like to have been hurt by someone else...

Because of all that we've done wrong, there's no way that we can go back to being perfect. How do you make something "imperfect" into something "perfect" again?

Well, for us humans, it's impossible! Only God could do something like that!

And, God DID do something like that, because into the Nation of Israel, 2,000 years ago, a child was born...

(2) THE BABY

A baby? Really? This whole story starts with a baby? Well, actually it doesn't! Confused yet? Just hold on because our story actually starts 500-700 years **before** this baby is born! (As I said, time travel isn't easy so we skipped going all the way back there, too!)

If we had traveled to around 2,500 years ago, we would have run into a man named Isaiah. Isaiah was what the Bible calls a "prophet"! Prophets were chosen **by** God to speak **for** God. Usually when God had to choose a prophet, it's because people were disobeying Him and hurting each other! Many times, when things got bad enough, God would send a prophet to a group of people and tell them to knock it off!

You see the Nation of Israel was supposed to be

following God. And they did...sometimes. When things were going bad, they spent a lot of time begging for God to save them. Then, when things were going well, they forgot about God. Prophets, like Isaiah, were sent by God to remind the people that they needed to make sure they were doing what God told them to do.

To help spread the word to the whole Nation of Israel, Isaiah wrote a book. That book talked about how great God was, the problems that Israel had, how they had refused to do what God said, and what was going to happen to them if they didn't start listening to God again!

But, in the middle of his book, Isaiah says something...weird:

> *All right then, the Lord himself will give you the sign. Look! The virgin will conceive a child! She will give birth to a son and will call him Immanuel (which means 'God is with us'). - Isaiah 7:14 (NLT)*

God, through Isaiah, says, "Hey Israel! Guess what? You aren't getting it, so I'm going to do something...impossible! I'm going to make a young woman become pregnant. And the Boy that's going to be born? That will be My Son! You are literally going to have 'God with you'!"

The people in Isaiah's time who read this said, "Whatever God! We're still going to do our own thing!" And time passed…

Then, 2,000 years ago, there was a young woman named Mary who was engaged to a man named Joseph. (Mary probably would have been around 12-years-old when she was engaged to Joseph, but that was pretty typical in those days.) Before they can get married, though, something happens! Let me show you:

This is how Jesus the Messiah was born. His mother, Mary, was engaged to be married to Joseph. But before the marriage took place, while she was still a virgin, she became pregnant through the power of the Holy Spirit. Joseph, to whom she was engaged, was a righteous man and did not want to disgrace her publicly, so he decided to break the engagement quietly.

As he considered this, an angel of the Lord appeared to him in a dream. "Joseph, son of David," the angel said, "do not be afraid to take Mary as your wife. For the child within her was conceived by the Holy Spirit. And she will have a son, and you are to name him Jesus, for he will save his people from their sins." - Matthew 1:18-21 (NLT)

So the very thing that Isaiah predicted 500 years

before…happens *exactly* like God said it would!

Matthew, the man who wrote these verses, must have read the Book of Isaiah at one point. Why? Because the very next thing Matthew says is:

> *All of this occurred to fulfill the Lord's message through his prophet: "Look! The virgin will conceive a child! She will give birth to a son, and they will call him Immanuel, which means 'God is with us.'" - Matthew 1:22-23 (NLT)*

Okay, now some of you are saying, "Predicting the future? A virgin having a child? Yep, sounds like a bunch of religious weirdos making up a bunch of crazy stuff!" It's easy to sit here 2,000 years later and say, "Wow! What a bunch of silly people!" (If that's you, I want you to know that I was once that way, too!)

It may surprise you, but I'm not going to argue with you or see if I can convince you to believe what I believe. Instead, let me explain why I think this story is true:

First, you have to know that Matthew, a very close follower of Jesus, believed it happened this way, which is why he wrote it down! Next, Luke, who was kind of like a detective, looked into the story, believed it was true, and then he also wrote it down! (Luke wrote the "Book of Luke" in the New Testament.)

For me, the reason that I think it's true is because Matthew and Luke, two very smart men who lived in that time, told me, "Hey! We know it's weird, but we researched it and this is exactly what happened, whether you believe it or not!"

Anyhow, let's get back to our story!

So Mary is pregnant and about to have a child, but there's a BIG problem! Do you remember when I was talking about how Rome actually ruled Israel? Well, one day they made a new law:

At that time the Roman emperor, Augustus, decreed that a census should be taken throughout the Roman Empire. (This was the first census taken when Quirinius was governor of Syria.) All returned to their own ancestral towns to register for this census. And because Joseph was a descendant of King David, he had to go to Bethlehem in Judea, David's ancient home. He traveled there from the village of Nazareth in Galilee. He took with him Mary, to whom he was engaged, who was now expecting a child. - Luke 2:1-5 (NLT)

Rome wanted to know how many people were living in their lands, so they took a census. We still do this in America today. Census-takers show up, count the people living in an area, and then it's done.

But Rome did their census in a very, very strange way! Instead of counting people where they lived, they made the people move back to the cities – and even countries! – their ancestors came from! (We have one record where the census took over 40 years to complete; and people were required to stay where they were the whole time!)

Joseph is the great-great - add a bunch more "greats" - grandchild of King David, one of Israel's greatest kings. Because of that, he needs to go back to David's hometown; a tiny little place called "Bethlehem"!

What do I mean by "tiny"? Well, it depends on who you listen to, but most experts that I've spoken with think that Bethlehem was a town with no more than 1,000 people living in it. In fact, quite a few books that I've read think that there were less than 300 people living there! (That's a pretty tiny town if you ask me!)

And this is the town that Joseph and Mary are heading to! By the way, Isaiah wasn't the only prophet who talked about Jesus before He was born; others did, too! A prophet named Micah says this about Jesus:

But you, O Bethlehem Ephrathah, are only a small village among all the people of Judah. Yet a ruler of Israel, whose origins are in the distant past, will come from you on my behalf. - Micah 5:2 (NLT)

Oh, and Micah was writing this prediction of Jesus about 700 years **before** Jesus actually showed up! Again, you don't have to believe that; however the people who followed Jesus sure did!

When Joseph and Mary arrive in Bethlehem, they try to find a place to stay. Since Bethlehem isn't a big city, there aren't many options. In fact, the Bible tells us:

And while they were there, the time came for her baby to be born. She gave birth to her firstborn son. She wrapped him snugly in strips of cloth and laid him in a manger, because there was no lodging available for them. - Luke 2:6-7 (NLT)

Okay, now I have to confess something. The first time I read this, I was confused! If this baby is supposed to be "God with us", God's own Son, then why does Mary have to give birth to Him in a barn, and then put Him in an animal's food dish? (That's what a manger is.)

But this story isn't done being confusing yet! Let me show you what happens next:

That night there were shepherds staying in the fields nearby, guarding their flocks of sheep. Suddenly, an angel of the Lord appeared among them, and the radiance of the Lord's glory surrounded them. They were terrified, but the angel reassured them. "Don't be afraid!" he said. "I bring you good news that will bring great joy to all people. The Savior—yes, the Messiah, the Lord—has been born today in Bethlehem, the city of David! And you will recognize him by this sign: You will find a baby wrapped snugly in strips of cloth, lying in a manger." - Luke 2:8-12 (NLT)

The first people told that Jesus was born were shepherds? In Israel, a shepherd was pretty much…unimportant! They weren't scientists, they weren't rock stars, and they weren't even very well-educated. In fact, most of the time, shepherds were simply…ignored.

Okay, what's really going on? This is so random and weird! Why would God pick a time and a place like this for Jesus to be born? I mean, shouldn't He be born in a palace, surrounded by rich people like kings and royalty?

Many years later, I learned that yes, Jesus should have had all of that! Instead, God is using a series of strange events to complete a story that began hundreds of years earlier and that also involved shepherds. That story is based on King

David, the ancestor of Jesus. Let me explain to you what I mean:

- David is a shepherd who is told that he is the new King of Israel...and, at the birth of Jesus, the shepherds are the first people told about the new King.

- David is out in the field, working, when someone comes to tell him that he's the new king...just like the shepherds were out in the fields, working, when the angels tell them about the new King!

- David is the least important person in his family...just like the shepherds were the least important people in their society!

- David receives a visit from a prophet, sent by God, announcing that he's the new king...just like the shepherds see angels, sent by God, to announce the birth of the new King!

- When Samuel (a prophet) announces that David is the new king, everyone is afraid...just like the shepherds were frightened when the angels showed up!

- We're told in the Bible that God's Spirit is

with David…and the angels tell the shepherds that God's Son is with them!

God likes to do things in a way that ties everything together! If we read the story of King David in 1 Samuel 16, there are a lot of things that it has in common with the story of his descendant, Jesus!

Now some of you may be sitting there and saying, "Wait! I've seen those Nativity things that people put out at Christmas! Weren't there three guys on camels that showed up to see the baby?"

Well, we're not really sure! We know some people showed up; but unfortunately we're not told exactly how many there were or even when they came!

This is a "Nativity Set" I bought when I was a teenager. It took many years for me to realize how wrong most of it is!

In Matthew chapter two, we find the story of the "Wise Men". They show up and go to Herod, the King of Israel, to ask where the new "King of the Jews" is. The Wise Men tell Herod that they have seen a new star in the night sky and they've followed it here, to Jerusalem!

There's a problem, though: as far as Herod knows, there isn't a new king! And if there *is* a new king, Herod wants him dead! (I told you King Herod wasn't a very nice guy!)

Anyhow, the religious leaders look up the Book of Micah that we talked about earlier, they see that Bethlehem is where the new king is to be born, and Herod comes up with a plan:

King Herod tells the men to go and find the child and then come back and tell him where the baby is. Herod explains to them that he wants to go worship this new king…but all he really wants to do is to kill anyone – even a baby boy – who might one day take his throne!

And what happens next?

After this interview the wise men went their way. And the star they had seen in the east guided them to Bethlehem. It went ahead of them and stopped over the place where the child was. When they saw the star, they were filled with joy! They entered the house and saw the child with his mother, Mary, and they bowed down and worshiped him. Then they opened their treasure chests and gave him gifts of gold, frankincense, and myrrh. - Matthew 2:9-11 (NLT)

So first things first: how many Wise Men are there? We're never told! There could have been three of them – most people think that because there are three gifts given. But, if these guys were astronomers from another country, they probably came with an entire caravan of people!

Second, where do they stop at? "They entered the house…" But where was Jesus born? In a barn! From that, a lot of people – myself included – think that they showed up later. How much later? It could actually have been around two years after Jesus was born!

Next, let's talk about their gifts. If you were choosing a gift for a newborn baby, you would probably think of stuff like rattles, diapers, blankets, and things like that. But these are a bunch of guys, and so what they bring is just...weird, in my opinion!

1. The first gift is gold. Gold is a GREAT gift to give to a newborn king! Overall, they did okay with this one!

2. The second gift is frankincense. Frankincense is a perfume (incense) that is burned by priests serving God. A priest is someone who stands between God and humans! Pretty important job; but why give this to a baby? Well, it actually does make sense if this baby really is "God with us". Who better to stand between God and us than His own Son? Okay, so maybe this one isn't such a bad gift, either!

3. The third gift is myrrh. Myrrh was used to cover dead bodies, especially if they were rich, important, or royalty. This gift is just a little bit creepy, if you ask me! Why would you ever give that to a baby boy...unless his death was going to be meaningful?

Well, let's keep going with the story and see what happens next:

When it was time to leave, they returned to their own country by another route, for God had warned them in a dream not to return to Herod. After the wise men were gone, an angel of the Lord appeared to Joseph in a dream. "Get up! Flee to Egypt with the child and his mother," the angel said. "Stay there until I tell you to return, because Herod is going to search for the child to kill him." - Matthew 2:12-13 (NLT)

I told you Herod wasn't such a great guy! When King Herod realizes that the Wise Men aren't coming back to him, he orders his soldier to kill every baby boy in and around Bethlehem that are two-years-old and younger. Herod isn't going to let **anyone** take his kingdom away from him!

Fortunately, Joseph, Mary, and Jesus have already escaped! Unfortunately for the other baby boys in the area, Herod is serious about killing everyone who might stand in the way of him and his power...

For those of us who follow Jesus, we celebrate the story of His birth every year. In fact, that's what "Christmas" literally means: "Christ Mass". This is a time for us to come together, to celebrate Jesus' birth, and to remember what He did for us. (We'll talk more about that later!)

In the United States, December 25th is "Christmas". And, while people have added a bunch of stuff to it – Christmas Trees, Santa Claus, and Snowmen – the true meaning of Christmas, the real reason that we celebrate, is because God gave US a gift! He gave us the gift of His Son, Jesus, to save us!

But that's getting ahead of my story; let's see what happens next!

(3) THE IN-BETWEEN

Now, we need to fast-forward to when Jesus turns thirty years old! Why are we skipping from "baby Jesus" to "adult Jesus"? Well, actually it's because we're not told much about what Jesus was like growing up!

It may seem strange, but there are only two main stories:

First, we're told in Luke chapter two that Jesus was taken to the Temple to be dedicated to God. Kind of strange to actually dedicate the Son of God TO God, but that was just part of living in Israel. (Luke 2:21-40)

Second, when Jesus was twelve, His parents took Him to Jerusalem for a special tradition called "Passover" – this is one of those festivals I mentioned earlier.

When they got ready to come back home, no one noticed that Jesus wasn't with them. When they realized He was missing, Jesus' parents returned to Jerusalem where they found Jesus, in the Temple, quizzing a bunch of religious leaders about God.

And, I LOVE what the Bible tells us about this twelve-year-old boy:

> *All who heard him were amazed at his understanding and his answers. - Luke 2:47 (NLT)*

Gee! Who would expect the Son of God to know more about God than a bunch of old guys who have spent their lives studying God? (I would!) You can check out that story in Luke 2:41-52.

Other than that, we simply don't know anything about Jesus beyond what would have been normal in His society. Jesus would have been a carpenter because that's what His earthly dad, Joseph, did. Jesus would have had brown-skin and dark hair, just like the other people in Israel at that time. Also, Jesus would have helped to take care of His family, like His brothers and sisters.

Oh, and there's one other thing that we can guess. After Luke 2, no one ever mentions Jesus' dad, Joseph, again. Because of that, most people who study the Bible think that Joseph dies while Jesus is growing up.

For me, I think Joseph is a pretty amazing guy! How hard would it be to raise the Son of God? I'm a parent, I have a son, and I still can't even **begin** to imagine how hard that would be! I'm kind of looking forward to seeing Joseph in Heaven and asking him what it was like.

And…that's it! I'm sorry this section is so short! But I hope you understand that it's not short because I don't think it's important; instead, it's short because the Bible just doesn't tell us that much about this time in Jesus' life!

(4) THE TEACHINGS

So we've skipped over Jesus' teen years, and now we get to meet Him when He's 30 years old! At this point, Jesus sets out from home and begins to teach everyone about who God is, what He's done, and what we should do because of Him. While this may not sound important, if Jesus really is "God with us", then we should probably pay attention to what Jesus says!

So what does Jesus say?

In the Book of Mark, Jesus is asked a simple question. Let me show you:

> *One of the teachers of religious law was standing there listening to the debate. He realized that Jesus had answered well, so he asked, "Of all the commandments, which is the most important?"*

Jesus replied, "The most important commandment is this: 'Listen, O Israel! The Lord our God is the one and only Lord. And you must love the Lord your God with all your heart, all your soul, all your mind, and all your strength.' The second is equally important: 'Love your neighbor as yourself.' No other commandment is greater than these." - Mark 12:28-31 (NLT)

So this guy comes up to Jesus and says, "Hey Jesus? Out of all of the rules in the Bible, which one is the most important? Is it, 'Don't murder people?' 'Don't spend your time wanting what other people have?' If you had to pick one thing, what would it be?"

What's Jesus' response?

Step One: Love God with everything you are.

Step Two: Love your neighbors like you love yourself.

In other words, we decide that we need God in our lives! And so we spend our time studying God, learning about Him, talking to Him (that's what it means to pray), and we learn to let God define us. That's Step One.

Step Two says that we take the love that God has for us and we show it to the people around us. We help them, encourage them, and let them know that we care about them, and that God cares about them, too!

Pretty simple stuff, right? The first step requires us to put God first in **everything** we do. The second step means that we spend our time treating others the way that we would want them to treat us. The crazy thing about this second step? We're supposed to do it even if the people around us aren't being nice to us!

To His audience, Jesus had to sound...crazy!

But that's only the first example! Let me show you what Jesus says to a guy named Peter:

> *Then Peter came to him and asked, "Lord, how often should I forgive someone who sins against me? Seven times?"*
>
> *"No, not seven times," Jesus replied, "but seventy times seven!" - Matthew 18:21-22 (NLT)*

Now, what you have to understand is that there's a crowd of people following Jesus around. Some are doing it because they can't wait to see what Jesus will do next; others are doing it because they want something from Him; and the last group follows Jesus because they think that He might be more than just an ordinary human.

In the middle of this crowd, there are twelve men called "The Twelve Disciples" or "The Twelve Apostles". These guys are Jesus' inner circle, His entourage. This group of men lives with Jesus, follows Jesus, learns from Jesus, and ultimately their goal is to go out and tell people about Jesus!

Peter is one of these guys. Peter also tries to impress Jesus by bragging about...himself. In this part of Matthew, Jesus has been talking about what to do if there are arguments between the people who follow Him.

Then Peter, to show Jesus that he's been listening and paying attention, says, "Hey Jesus? How often do you think I should forgive someone who has hurt me? I've been thinking about this, and I think I should do it...like...seven times! Pretty good, right? Seven times I'll forgive them! That's just how amazing I am! What do you think?"

Jesus looks at Peter, shakes His head, and says, "Yeah, not quite. Try forgiving someone seventy times seven!"

Before I explain the rest of this, you need to understand that Jesus doesn't mean you **only** have to forgive someone 490 times. (I use the term "only" in a slightly ironic fashion.) What He means is that there shouldn't be a limit on how much we're willing to forgive.

Peter's attempt at figuring out what Jesus meant. (We'll ignore the fact that they didn't have calculators, markers, or even paper!)

Now, if you're like me, this may bother you. I was hurt very badly by someone, and it made me angry enough to want to hurt him back! In fact, I spent part of my life planning on HOW I was going to do it! But then I found out that Jesus told me to let the guy go! How fair is that?

Well, actually Jesus told me to do it for my own good! You see, I spent years of my life thinking about this guy, replaying what he did in my head, focusing on how he hurt me, staying angry, being afraid, and more! This guy – who probably never thought about me after that – was taking up a whole lot of my time and my thoughts!

Then, when I learned how to really forgive that man, I found out that I wasn't angry anymore! I wasn't afraid. I learned that I could have peace! Even more important, I gave up my desire to hurt him. Instead, I got to leave him in God's hands; to let God do what He wanted with the man. And me? I got to go…free!

If you've been hurt by other people, the best advice I can give you is to learn to forgive. If you do, you'll find that it helps you every bit as much as it helps them…or maybe even MORE than it helps them!

Okay, let's go to another spot:

> *"Do not judge others, and you will not be judged. Do not condemn others, or it will all come back against you. Forgive others, and you will be forgiven." - Luke 6:37 (NLT)*

Now a lot of people get this verse wrong. They say, "See? Christians can't judge others!" But Jesus also tells us in Luke 6:43-45 that we're supposed to be able to tell a "good tree" from a "bad one". How can we do that if we can't judge what's "good" and "bad"?

Actually, the better way to say this is, "Don't be judge, jury, and executioner!" In other words, I don't get to look at someone else and say, "God hates you!" or "Your mistakes are bigger than my mistakes!" or "I'm a better person than you are!"

A gavel used in a courtroom by a judge.

Instead, I look at my own life first and work on fixing what's wrong. Next, I look at the lives of the people around me and try to help them work on areas where they're having problems. I don't yell at them; I feel sorry for them and reach out to them.

Before we wrap up this chapter, let's look at one more thing that Jesus said:

> *Jesus told him, "I am the way, the truth, and the life. No one can come to the Father except through me. If you had really known me, you would know who my Father is. From now on, you do know him and have seen him!" - John 14:6-7 (NLT)*

Now a lot of people in America today don't like this statement! I've had people tell me, "All religions lead to God!" "You're just excluding people!" "God will accept me no matter what I believe!" And, if Jesus IS NOT the Son of God, then those things **may** be true.

But, what if Jesus IS the Son of God? If He is, then that means that Jesus and God have the same nature!

Let me explain this idea in a simple way: Human parents have human children. Fish parents have fishy children. Eagle parents have baby eagles. The babies all have the same nature and the same characteristics as the parents, right?

So, if Jesus **is** the Son of God, then He would **be** God. And if that's true, if Jesus really is God, and Jesus tells us that the only way to get to God is by believing in Him, then if we don't believe in Jesus, we have a HUGE problem!

By the way, this isn't the only place where Jesus claims to be God. While He never directly says, "I am God!" there are a lot of times when Jesus – and others – make statements that mean the same thing.

If you want to see more examples, go read:

- John 1:14 (John, a follower of Jesus, says that Jesus is God.

- John 8:58 ("I Am" is the name God gives to Himself.)

- John 10:30 ("Father" is another title for God.)

Also, there are a bunch of other places where the people who followed Jesus told everyone that Jesus was God. And the reason they could say this? Because they were convinced, based on everything they heard and saw, that Jesus and God are the same person!

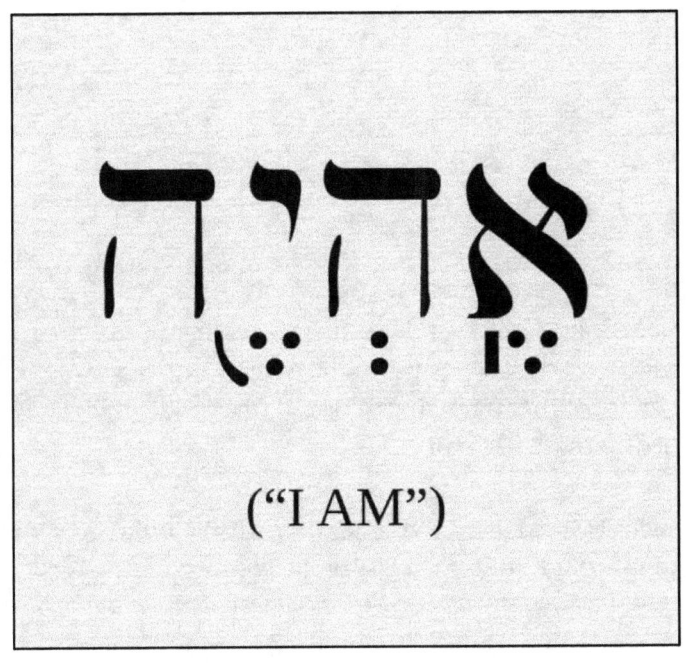

("I AM")

If you want to understand the meaning of
"I Am", read Exodus 3:13-15!

(5) THE MIRACLES

So we've seen how Jesus was born, how He was raised, and we've talked about what He taught to the crowds of people following Him. Now, we get into the part that a lot of people have BIG problems with: miracles.

Just so you know, the Merriam-Webster Dictionary defines a miracle as, *"an extraordinary event manifesting divine intervention in human affairs"*.

In other words, things are going along normally and *Bam!* God steps in, changes the rules, and something incredible happens! And we need to remember that if God made the rules, He has the ability to change them!

Now, as I read through the stories of the miracles of Jesus, I look at them in a different way than most people. You see, my hobby is magic tricks. I can pull a rabbit out of a hat, cause books to burst into flames, and I can even read your mind! (Spooky, right?)

The one thing that you have to know is that ALL of these are just...tricks. Like I tell the groups I perform for, "Nothing you see tonight is real. All of it's fake; and if you had a few thousand dollars to buy the tricks and a few months to learn them, then you could do everything I do!"

So when I sit down and read the miracles that Jesus did, I look for ways that I could do it. And do you know what I've found? I learned that if I had $500,000 to buy supplies, two semi-trucks to carry the gear, and about a week of time to prep, I actually COULD do some of the "miracles".

For example, I could turn water into wine, I could feed 5,000 people, and I could even heal a man who was paralyzed! It would all be tricks, of course!

- To turn water into wine, I could have powdered "wine" that I could mix with jars of water. (If I don't have to let you get too close, I have another way to do it that looks good, but involves some very toxic chemicals!)

- For feeding 5,000 people, I could hide supplies of food in holes that I covered with rocks. My Disciples – my followers – could put their baskets onto these rocks, reach through a secret hole in the bottom, move the rock, find the food underneath, pull it out, and then move the rock back over the hole.

- To heal someone who was paralyzed, I would simply get someone who was NOT paralyzed and have them pretend. Since no one would know if the guy was paralyzed or not, we could fake it and see if anyone believed us.

My "Water-To-Wine" Trick, complete with lethal chemicals!

And if those were the only "miracles" that Jesus did, then there's no way that I could ever believe in Him. Why? Because I could copy everything that He did using simple magic tricks!

Now, to be fair, Jesus didn't have weeks of time to set these up. He also didn't have semi-trucks to haul the gear around. (Remember this is about 1,900 years before semi-trucks were even invented!) I'm also willing to bet that a guy who worked as a carpenter didn't have tons of money lying around to buy the supplies!

Also, there's the problem of the miracles that His followers described that I can't do... Let me show you what I mean:

> *Then Jesus got into the boat and started across the lake with his disciples. Suddenly, a fierce storm struck the lake, with waves breaking into the boat. But Jesus was sleeping. The disciples went and woke him up, shouting, "Lord, save us! We're going to drown!"*
>
> *Jesus responded, "Why are you afraid? You have so little faith!" Then he got up and rebuked the wind and waves, and suddenly there was a great calm.*
>
> *The disciples were amazed. "Who is this man?" they asked. "Even the winds and waves obey him!"*
> *- Matthew 8:23-27 (NLT)*

Did you notice who wrote this story down? It's found in the Book of Matthew, so Matthew is the one who wrote it, right? And do you want to know where Matthew was when this miracle took place? He was out on the lake, in the middle of the storm, in a boat that was starting to sink!

This isn't a story that someone told to someone who heard it from someone else! Matthew is right there and he's one of the people who called out to Jesus to save him!

When Jesus wakes up, what's His response? He looks at His Disciples and says, "Why are you worried about something this small?" Then Jesus tells the storm, "Knock it off!" And it does!

The Bible doesn't say, but I'm assuming that after the storm stops, Jesus curls back up to finish His nap. That leaves the Disciples – the followers of Jesus – to sit around and ask themselves how any **human** could command the weather!

In the Book of Mark, we find a different story:

> *Jesus went into the synagogue again and noticed a man with a deformed hand. Since it was the Sabbath, Jesus' enemies watched him closely. If he healed the man's hand, they planned to accuse him of working on the Sabbath.*

Jesus said to the man with the deformed hand, "Come and stand in front of everyone." Then he turned to his critics and asked, "Does the law permit good deeds on the Sabbath, or is it a day for doing evil? Is this a day to save life or to destroy it?" But they wouldn't answer him.

He looked around at them angrily and was deeply saddened by their hard hearts. Then he said to the man, "Hold out your hand." So the man held out his hand, and it was restored! At once the Pharisees went away and met with the supporters of Herod to plot how to kill Jesus. - Mark 3:1-6 (NLT)

The religious people in Israel had a rule: you couldn't work on the Sabbath. (The Sabbath is kind of like our Sunday in America.) God told everyone to take a day off, but the religious leaders spent a lot of time trying to figure out what was "work" and what wasn't!

So, when He's in the synagogue – which is kind of like a church – and sees a man with a deformed hand, Jesus is going to use the situation to teach the religious leaders a lesson.

Basically, Jesus asks them, "Which is more important: to obey all of the rules that you've come up with…or to obey God? Should I NOT help this guy because I want you all to like

Me? Or, do I help this guy because God loves him?"

How do you answer that? If you say, "Keep our rules and let this guy suffer!" you look like jerks; especially since they're YOUR rules! If you say, "I guess you can break our rules this one time!" then why do you have rules in the first place? Either way, anything the religious leaders say is going to make them look silly; so they say nothing at all!

Jesus, who knows what they're thinking, feels sorry for them…and then heals the man, anyhow!

But I want you to notice the reaction of the religious leaders here! They don't say, "Hey! That guy didn't have a deformed hand!" They don't say, "Hey! Medical doctors came in and healed his hand!" In fact, they don't argue *at all* about the fact that a miracle has happened! (It's pretty convincing proof when even the people who don't like you think you did a miracle!)

Instead, the religious leaders are so mad that Jesus made them look silly that they decide to kill Him! Wow! Jesus does a miracle, and they want Him dead because of it…

Oh, and speaking of how people reacted to Jesus

doing miracles, let's look at the Book of Luke:

As Jesus continued on toward Jerusalem, he reached the border between Galilee and Samaria. As he entered a village there, ten men with leprosy stood at a distance, crying out, "Jesus, Master, have mercy on us!"

He looked at them and said, "Go show yourselves to the priests." And as they went, they were cleansed of their leprosy.

One of them, when he saw that he was healed, came back to Jesus, shouting, "Praise God!" He fell to the ground at Jesus' feet, thanking him for what he had done. This man was a Samaritan.

Jesus asked, "Didn't I heal ten men? Where are the other nine? Has no one returned to give glory to God except this foreigner?" And Jesus said to the man, "Stand up and go. Your faith has healed you." - Luke 17:11-19 (NLT)

The first thing you have to understand is that leprosy is a terrible disease, even with the medical treatments we have today. Leprosy is contagious and can cause nerve damage, crippling of the hands and feet, and loss of fingers and toes! Nowadays, we can kill the bacteria that cause leprosy with antibiotics, but we still can't reverse the damage.

In Jesus' time, though, there was no cure. What most countries did was take the people with leprosy and kick them out of their society! You couldn't come into the towns, you couldn't have direct contact with other people, and you usually didn't have a family or friends. Why? It was just too contagious, too risky!

Even worse, you didn't have to have leprosy to be banished! Because they didn't have the medical knowledge that we do today, they called most skin conditions "leprosy" and, if you had **any** of them, they kicked you out just to be safe!

One of the "early" signs of leprosy is blotchy skin, ranging from white to dark. This allowed people to see - from a distance! - that you were infected!

Jesus, on His way to Jerusalem, the main city in Israel, runs into ten men with leprosy! They stand at a distance and call out to Him to heal them...and Jesus does.

One of the ten runs back and thanks Jesus for healing them. As for the other nine? They go away, get checked out by the priests, and then rejoin their society. They never once bother to say "Thank You".

But Jesus healed them not because He wanted them to thank Him; He did it because He loved them, felt sorry for them, and wanted them to be whole.

Okay, I've saved the best for last. Mary, Martha, and Lazarus are all friends with Jesus; but there's a problem: Lazarus is sick and dying! An even bigger problem is that Jesus has enemies that have decided that if He comes to help Lazarus, they're going to try to kill Him! By the time Jesus shows up, Lazarus is dead...

Jesus had stayed outside the village, at the place where Martha met him. When the people who were at the house consoling Mary saw her leave so hastily, they assumed she was going to Lazarus's grave to weep. So they followed her there. When Mary arrived and saw Jesus, she fell at his feet and said, "Lord, if only you had been here, my brother would not have died."

When Jesus saw her weeping and saw the other

people wailing with her, a deep anger welled up within him, and he was deeply troubled. "Where have you put him?" he asked them.

They told him, "Lord, come and see." Then Jesus wept. The people who were standing nearby said, "See how much he loved him!" But some said, "This man healed a blind man. Couldn't he have kept Lazarus from dying?"

Jesus was still angry as he arrived at the tomb, a cave with a stone rolled across its entrance. "Roll the stone aside," Jesus told them.

But Martha, the dead man's sister, protested, "Lord, he has been dead for four days. The smell will be terrible."

Jesus responded, "Didn't I tell you that you would see God's glory if you believe?" So they rolled the stone aside. Then Jesus looked up to heaven and said, "Father, thank you for hearing me. You always hear me, but I said it out loud for the sake of all these people standing here, so that they will believe you sent me." Then Jesus shouted, "Lazarus, come out!" And the dead man came out, his hands and feet bound in graveclothes, his face wrapped in a headcloth. Jesus told them, "Unwrap him and let him go!" - John 11:30-44 (NLT)

Okay, the first thing you need to know is that this

is a longer story than what I put in this book. If you want to read the whole thing for yourself, go check out John 11:1-44. (By the way, if you want to see the response of the religious leaders to this miracle, be sure to read the rest of the chapter, too!)

Jesus shows up, He sees the people crying, and He feels sorry for them. This isn't a "god" who doesn't care! Jesus shows that God is listening, that God hurts when we hurt!

Even more than that, Jesus gets angry because this world was never supposed to hurt people! Death, sickness, disease, and pain all came when we humans told God that we didn't want Him or need Him around!

When we decided to go our own way, we gave up a perfect relationship with God and, instead, we chose...pain! (Seems like a dumb trade, right?)

But Jesus is going to show the people who is really in control of...everything! When Jesus calls a dead man to get up, he does! Even death can't stop God! (Someone once pointed out to me that if Jesus hadn't said, "LAZARUS, come out!" the whole graveyard – everyone who had died! – would have come to life again!)

So, where does this leave us? Today, as we talk

about miracles, I want to show you what a miracle looks like through the eyes of a magician; someone trained to deceive (or trick) people. (Kind of a cool job description, right?)

Like I said, I can copy some of Jesus' miracles with simple magic tricks. But calming a storm? Healing someone? Bringing the dead back to life? Not a chance!

More importantly, the people who followed Jesus, His Disciples, believed in these miracles so much that they wrote them down!

Finally, even the people who hated Jesus didn't argue that He was doing miracles. They were just upset because Jesus wasn't doing them the way they thought He should!

A scientist and atheist (someone who doesn't believe God exists) named Carl Sagan once said: *"Extraordinary claims require extraordinary evidence!"* In other words, if someone is claiming supernatural abilities, they had better be able to back it up.

In the New Testament, the second half of the Bible, Jesus goes around telling people that He's the Son of God. Even more than that, Jesus claimed that He **was** God! (That's a HUGE claim, just in case you weren't sure!) To back it up, to prove that He was who He said He was, Jesus does some HUGE miracles!

Every time Jesus claimed to be the Son of God, people wanted proof. And Jesus healed the sick. And Jesus fed the crowds. And Jesus raised people from the dead. *"Extraordinary claims require extraordinary evidence."* And that's what Jesus does: He provides extraordinary evidence!

There have been others in history who claimed to be God. Do you want to know how many miracles they pulled off? None. Do you want to know how many times their enemies said, "Yeah, we agree that this person is doing miracles!"? Never. Because of that, Jesus is unique.

But there's one last miracle we need to talk about, and this one is simply…impossible!

(6) THE PASSOVER

To get to this last miracle, we need to go to "church". Well, not exactly...

For Jewish people, their version of a church was called a "synagogue". The word "synagogue" means *"a bringing together"*. In other words, the synagogue was a place where people gathered together to talk about God, to learn more about what God said, and synagogues were also used for trials and punishments. The other thing to point out is that synagogues met on Saturday (the "Sabbath"), not on Sunday, like most churches in America do. (To keep it all simple, though, we're going to say that synagogues are like churches.)

In the Bible, we find that Jesus went into the synagogues to teach. For example, we find in Luke 4:

When [Jesus] came to the village of Nazareth, his boyhood home, he went as usual to the synagogue on the Sabbath and stood up to read the Scriptures. The scroll of Isaiah the prophet was handed to him. He unrolled the scroll and found the place where this was written:

"The Spirit of the Lord is upon me, for he has anointed me to bring Good News to the poor. He has sent me to proclaim that captives will be released, that the blind will see, that the oppressed will be set free, and that the time of the Lord's favor has come."

He rolled up the scroll, handed it back to the attendant, and sat down. All eyes in the synagogue looked at him intently. Then he began to speak to them. "The Scripture you've just heard has been fulfilled this very day!" - Luke 4:16-21 (NLT)

Notice what Jesus says here? He reads from the Book of Isaiah – the same book that talks about how a child would be born who is 'God with us' – and, in this part, Isaiah says that "the time of the Lord's favor has come".

Jesus finishes reading, looks at the crowd gathered there, and then He says, "Have you heard this before? Well, just in case you were wondering, that time is now! Why? Because I, the Son of God, am here!" That's a pretty bold statement…unless it's true!

Now, besides the synagogues, the Nation of Israel also had a central "church" called "The Temple". The Temple was located in Jerusalem, the capital of Israel. It was here that most people in Israel went for some of the bigger celebrations!

And the most important celebration of all? The Passover!

To explain what Passover is, we need to go back in time again; only now we have to travel 3,500 years from our modern time! We also need to go to a foreign land that you've probably heard about: Egypt. (Yep, the country with the pyramids, pharaohs, and the Sphinx!)

In Egypt 3,500 years ago, lived…the Egyptians! (I know! Surprising, right?) But there also lived another group of people: the Nation of Israel!

To explain this, you need to know something about the Middle East; and about other countries, in general. In America, most people have enough food to eat. Not all do, but most.

In the Middle East – in countries like Egypt, Israel, and Moab – you raised your own food. If there was a drought (it didn't rain for a long time), or if there were swarms of locusts (big clouds of bugs), or if your land was attacked, you couldn't farm! If you couldn't farm, then you couldn't get enough food. If you couldn't get enough food, you and your family starved.

Egypt, complete with pyramids and a caravan on camels!

At one point, in the Book of Genesis, there was a famine in the land. Only Egypt had food, and they only had food because God had put someone there to help them out! If you want a great story, go read about Joseph in Genesis chapters 37 through 46!

The Nation of Israel, only a few families at this time, moved down to Egypt to live because there was food. The Pharaoh, or ruler, of Egypt, thankful to Joseph for saving his people, gave these families a safe place to stay. During that time, the Nation of Israel lived as honored guests in the land.

But, after a while, new pharaohs came into power. These men looked at the Nation of Israel and said, "You know what? There are a lot of them! If we're not careful, they could attack us and take over our country!" And so one of these Egyptian rulers, a man who didn't know anything about the story of Joseph, forced the Nation of Israel to become his slaves!

After centuries of living in slavery – a time in which they were starved, beaten, forced to work, and were even killed! – God sent a man named Moses to get the current Pharaoh to set the Nation of Israel free.

Some of you might have heard about the "Ten Plagues of Egypt". If not, and you want another great story to read, check out Exodus chapters 3 through 14.

The final plague described in Exodus 11 is the one that I want to talk about here: the death of the firstborn. Let me show you:

Moses had announced to Pharaoh, "This is what the LORD says: At midnight tonight I will pass through the heart of Egypt. All the firstborn sons will die in every family in Egypt, from the oldest son of Pharaoh, who sits on his throne, to the oldest son of his lowliest servant girl who grinds the flour. Even the firstborn of all the livestock will die. Then a loud wail will rise throughout the land of Egypt, a wail like no one has heard before or will ever hear again. But among the Israelites it will be so peaceful that not even a dog will bark. Then you will know that the LORD makes a distinction between the Egyptians and the Israelites. All the officials of Egypt will run to me and fall to the ground before me. 'Please leave!' they will beg. 'Hurry! And take all your followers with you.' Only then will I go!" Then, burning with anger, Moses left Pharaoh. - Exodus 11:4-8 (NLT)

Pharaoh has had nine other chances to let the Nation of Israel go free. Nine times he hasn't cared about what the plagues have done to his people or to his kingdom.

More than once, Pharaoh has said, "If you end this plague, I'll let you go free!" Then, when Moses asked God to end the plague, Pharaoh basically said, "Ha! I lied to you! Now that the plague is over, your people are still slaves!"

This time, the plague that's coming is so terrible that the entire Nation of Egypt is going to beg

Israel to leave! In fact, God basically says to Egypt, "Okay! You thought you could lie to My people? You thought I wasn't serious? Game on! What I'm about to do in your land will terrify everyone who hears it! You will become a story, a legend; something that will frighten not just little children, but adults, too! Other countries will hear My people coming and they will run away because of what I'm about to do to you!"

I don't know about you, but if God told me that what was about to happen to me would be enough to scare people hundreds of miles away who only hear of it, I think I would run away!

Moses then goes to Israel and tells them what they need to do to be safe:

> *Then Moses called all the elders of Israel together and said to them, "Go, pick out a lamb or young goat for each of your families, and slaughter the Passover animal. Drain the blood into a basin. Then take a bundle of hyssop branches and dip it into the blood. Brush the hyssop across the top and sides of the doorframes of your houses. And no one may go out through the door until morning. For the LORD will pass through the land to strike down the Egyptians. But when he sees the blood on the top and sides of the doorframe, the LORD will pass over your home. He will not permit his death angel to enter*

your house and strike you down." - Exodus 12:21-23 (NLT)

In other words, to be set free from slavery, to be saved from death, they were to kill a perfect lamb, and use its blood as paint around the doors of their houses. When God moved through the land of Egypt, the blood would be a sign to skip that house; the people inside were protected, they were saved, by the blood of the lamb!

That night, God did just what He said He was going to do:

> *So the people of Israel did just as the LORD had commanded through Moses and Aaron. And that night at midnight, the LORD struck down all the firstborn sons in the land of Egypt, from the firstborn son of Pharaoh, who sat on his throne, to the firstborn son of the prisoner in the dungeon. Even the firstborn of their livestock were killed. Pharaoh and all his officials and all the people of Egypt woke up during the night, and loud wailing was heard throughout the land of Egypt. There was not a single house where someone had not died. - Exodus 12:28-30 (NLT)*

As a result of this, Israel is set free and – eventually – they make it to the land God promised them! (A lot happens in between, but we don't have time to cover that here!)

Also, from this time on, Israel began a religious ritual where they would sacrifice animals – usually lambs – to try to cover up their mistakes, what the Bible calls "sins". And, even in Jesus' day, they were still sacrificing animals to try to cover their sins.

The "Passover Lamb"

Oh, and like I mentioned at the start, the city of Jerusalem, where the Temple was at, would triple in size when the Nation of Israel came together to celebrate Passover!

Okay, so what am I doing here? I started this chapter by talking about synagogues (basically a Jewish church), I talked about the Temple (the central place of religion for the Jews), and then I talked about the history of Passover. What does any of this have to do with the history of Jesus?

Well, it all comes down to two short passages, or parts, of the Bible:

In the Book of John, Jesus goes out to see a man named John the Baptist. (John the Baptist isn't the guy who wrote the Book of John! "John" was a common name back then.) When John the Baptist sees Jesus coming, he says this:

> *The next day John saw Jesus coming toward him and said, "Look! The Lamb of God who takes away the sin of the world!" - John 1:29 (NLT)*

John sees Jesus and how does he describe Him? The Lamb of God. In other words, John calls Jesus, "The Passover Lamb".

Also, according to the rules for Passover, to take away your sins the Passover Lamb has to be perfect. So, Jesus comes to earth and lives a perfect life. Jesus never sins, never makes a mistake, and always does what God wants because He is "God with us"!

Finally, what did you do to the Passover Lamb to be saved from your sins? You had to kill them, remember?

Then, if we go to Luke 22, we see this:

> *The Festival of Unleavened Bread, which is also called Passover, was approaching. The leading priests and teachers of religious law were plotting how to kill Jesus, but they were afraid of the people's reaction.*
>
> *Then Satan entered into Judas Iscariot, who was one of the twelve disciples, and he went to the leading priests and captains of the Temple guard to discuss the best way to betray Jesus to them. They were delighted, and they promised to give him money. So he agreed and began looking for an opportunity to betray Jesus so they could arrest him when the crowds weren't around. - Luke 22:1-6 (NLT)*

At Passover time, one of Jesus' Disciples, one of His followers, agrees to sell out Jesus. Judas will betray Jesus to the religious leaders. After He's arrested, the religious leaders will have a trial for Him; and, because of this, Jesus – the Passover Lamb, the perfect sacrifice – will be sentenced to die.

We'll get to more of that in a moment, but there are a couple of things we need to talk about first!

(7) THE DEATH

Depending on who you hang out with, you may have seen people wearing a cross around their neck. For some, it may be a plain cross; while others may have a man on the cross. Most people who wear a necklace like that have learned something about Jesus. They may not actually **believe** in Jesus – their family might have bought the necklace for them – but they probably **know** something about Jesus!

And, in this chapter, we need to talk about why that type of jewelry exists.

When we last left Jesus, He had been betrayed. Soon, He will be put on trial and sentenced to death! His Disciples, His followers, will run away and go into hiding. Jesus will be on His own, and He will be preparing to die. But, there's a catch to this... (Isn't there always?)

Remember, who actually runs the Nation of Israel at this time? Rome! And while the religious leaders could recommend that someone be killed, the only people who could actually do it were the Romans!

Not that the Romans had a problem killing people! In fact, if you did anything Rome didn't like, they would happily kill you! Sometimes they would kill you quickly, like by beheading. Other times, they would kill you slowly; like sending you far away and letting you die alone. And, if they really didn't like you, they would crucify you!

What does "crucify" mean? Well, we'll get to that shortly. Let's talk about what happened after Jesus is sentenced to death by the religious leaders:

> Then the entire council took Jesus to Pilate, the Roman governor. They began to state their case: "This man has been leading our people astray by telling them not to pay their taxes to the Roman government and by claiming he is the Messiah, a king." - Luke 23:1-2 (NLT)

What's funny about these charges is...they aren't really true.

- In Luke 20:25, Jesus says, "Give to Caesar what belongs to Caesar". In other words, if the coin you're using has Caesar's picture on it, then give it to him, since it's his! But, Jesus then goes on to say, "And give to God what is God's". Well, since God owns everything, then everything belongs to God, right?

- In Luke 9:21, Jesus tells His Disciples not to call Him "The Messiah". He doesn't say, "I'm NOT the Messiah!" Instead, Jesus says, "Don't tell everyone about it! There's a lot of work to be done to prove that I'm the Savior, the King you're waiting for!"

So Jesus didn't say "don't pay taxes" and "I'm the Messiah". But here's the weird part: because Jesus also doesn't come right out and say "pay taxes" and "I'm not the Messiah", it's enough to accuse Him!

To help you understand this, it's like saying to you, "Because you haven't openly said, 'I am not an alien', you MUST be an alien bent on world conquest!" Because Jesus hasn't said the exact words, it's enough of a gray area for the religious leaders to drag him before the Roman Governor! (I don't know about you, but I think that logic is kind of weird!)

Now, if you're the Roman Governor, a man named Pontius Pilate, can you have someone going around speaking out against Rome? No! If you allowed it, not only would the person saying things against Rome be killed; but you would be killed, too, just for letting them do it!

Pilate, though, doesn't really like the religious leaders. We find out from historians outside the Bible that the religious leaders had reported Pilate to Rome for a lot of trivial stuff. Because they hate each other, Pilate doesn't want Jesus to be killed.

So, Pilate sends Jesus to Herod Antipas, one of the children of Herod the Great, the man who killed the babies at the start of our story! That doesn't work out so well, and Antipas sends Jesus back to Pilate.

Pilate then tries another option:

> *Then Pilate called together the leading priests and other religious leaders, along with the people, and he announced his verdict. "You brought this man to me, accusing him of leading a revolt. I have examined him thoroughly on this point in your presence and find him innocent. Herod came to the same conclusion and sent him back to us. Nothing this man has done calls for the death penalty. So I will have him flogged, and then I will release him."*

- Luke 23:13-16 (NLT)

Pilate says, "Hey! I don't think this Jesus has done anything wrong. So, instead of killing Him, I'm going to have Him whipped and then let Him go free!"

But this doesn't work out so well, either. In Mark 15, we're told that the religious leaders have the crowd call for Jesus to be crucified. This may not seem like a big deal to us, but if you disobeyed the religious leaders, they could kick you out of the Temple and the synagogues! That's a pretty big threat, so the people did what they were told and chanted, "Crucify Him!"

Now some of you may be sitting there and saying, "What does it mean to be crucified?" Well, I'm going to talk about it in general terms, but I'm going to skip some of the really gory details, okay? If you want to learn more, there are a lot of books that talk about the parts that I'm going to skip!

Step One: Whipping
The first thing that happened to Jesus is the whipping:

So to pacify the crowd, Pilate released Barabbas to them. He ordered Jesus flogged with a lead-tipped whip, then turned him over to the Roman

73

soldiers to be crucified. - Mark 15:15 (NLT)

If you've ever seen pictures of slaves in American history, you might have seen what it looked like to be whipped. It's pretty nasty! But the Roman whips were worse than those used on African slaves! In fact, it was so bad that a lot of people died from the whipping, itself!

Step Two: Carrying The Cross
The next thing we're going to talk about is Jesus carrying the cross:

> *Along the way, they came across a man named Simon, who was from Cyrene, and the soldiers forced him to carry Jesus' cross. - Matthew 27:32 (NLT)*

The person sentenced to death was forced to carry a large, wooden cross to the place where they were going to be killed. While there's some debate on this, a lot of experts think Jesus didn't carry the whole cross like pictures show. Instead, He had to carry the horizontal beam which could have weighed between 50-100 pounds.

In fact, Jesus, weakened by lack of sleep, a false trial, and a brutal whipping, can't carry the beam on His own. When He falls, the

Roman soldiers grab a man named Simon and force him to carry the heavy weight the rest of the way.

Step Three: The Nails

The next step is the nails:

> *There they nailed him to the cross. Two others were crucified with him, one on either side, with Jesus between them. - John 19:18 (NLT)*

In my office, I have a replica, a copy, of one of these nails and it's close to eight inches long!

One of these nails would have been pounded through each of Jesus' wrists. (The Romans considered the wrist to be a part of the hand.) Then, they would have crossed Jesus' ankles over each other and driven a third one into His feet!

Step Four: The Death

While hanging on the cross, Jesus would have had to push Himself up on the nails to be able to breathe. Then He would slide back down the rough, wooden beams to relax. He would do this over and over again. In fact, the way crucifixion worked, you couldn't decide to **not** breathe and die quickly because the body would drag itself up to gasp for air, whether you wanted to keep living or not!

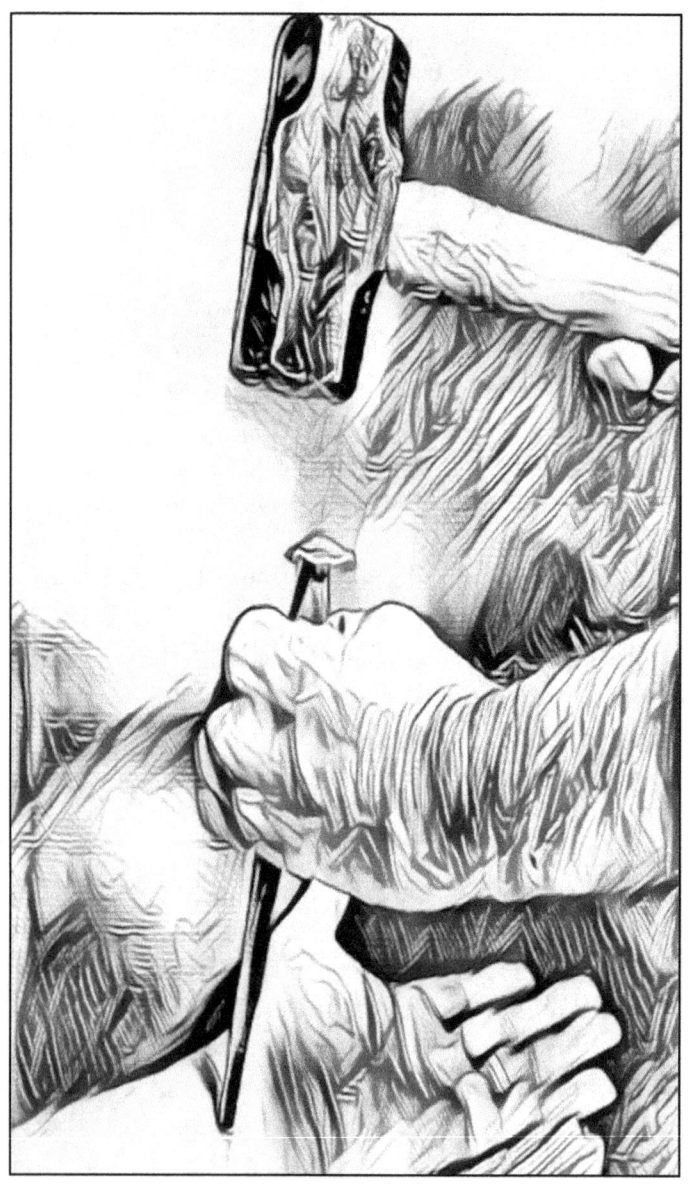

The nails being driven in.

This way of dying was so horrible, so painful, that the Romans had to invent an entirely new word for it: "excruciating". The word excruciating literally means "out of the cross". (You know it's got to be horrible if you have to invent new words to describe how badly people suffered, right?)

And Jesus hangs like this, in terrible pain, until He dies…

Step Five: The Proof
To make sure Jesus died, there is one final proof:

> *But when they came to Jesus, they saw that he was already dead, so they didn't break his legs. One of the soldiers, however, pierced his side with a spear, and immediately blood and water flowed out. (This report is from an eyewitness giving an accurate account. He speaks the truth so that you also may continue to believe.) - John 19:33-35 (NLT)*

The Roman soldier, not sure if Jesus was really dead, shoved a spear up into His side. John tells us that an eyewitness, someone who was right there, saw it happen! And why did John write that down? So that we could all be sure that Jesus was dead! Completely, totally, dead.

Just so you know, I did skip over a lot of other pieces. The writers of the Gospels – Matthew, Mark, Luke, and John – wrote more in their books about the crucifixion. If the stuff I talked about seemed pretty gruesome, there is a lot worse in the details I *didn't* talk about!

The other thing you need to know is that people NOT in the Bible wrote about Jesus dying by crucifixion, too! A Roman historian named Tacitus said this about Jesus:

> *"Nero fastened the guilt and inflicted the most exquisite tortures on a class hated for their abominations, called Christians by the populace. Christus, from whom the name had its origin, suffered the extreme penalty [Crucifixion] during the reign of Tiberius at the hands of our procurators, Pontius Pilatus..." (Source: Tacitus, Annals 15.44)*

In other words, even the Romans knew that Jesus had been crucified and died under Pontius Pilate!

So some Jewish guy gets killed by Rome 2,000 years ago! Big deal, right? That happened a lot, so why should this man be any different? Actually, if this was the end of the story, it wouldn't be a big deal at all!

The other question is why would Jesus, if He

really was the Son of God, let someone put Him through that sort of ordeal? That was something I wanted to know when I first heard about this!

But before we get there, let's look at one more detail in this story!

(8) THE BURIAL

For everything we've covered to make sense, you need to understand three things:

<u>First, Jesus lived.</u>
There are some people who argue that there never was a guy named "Jesus" in the first place. Do they base this idea on "science"? Nope. It's just their opinion, and most of the time it doesn't even make sense!

We have the writings from the Bible that tell the story of Jesus. We have writings from the early church, and some of those people saw Jesus. Finally, we have Roman and Jewish sources that confirm parts of the story of Jesus. All-in-all, it would take a lot to say, "Despite all of that proof that's out there, Jesus wasn't a real person!" But I want you to know there ARE some people who say that!

<u>Second, Jesus died.</u>
Like the first fact, there are some people who say this was made up, too. Again, we have the writings of the Bible, the early church, and the Romans to back this one up. Even more than that, pretty much everyone agrees that, if Jesus lived, He died at some point. I think, based on the evidence, Jesus died by crucifixion under the Roman Governor, Pontius Pilate.

<u>Third, Jesus was buried.</u>
Again, this should normally come next, based on the first two points. If you're dead, you get buried. Since Jesus died, logically He would be buried.

At this point, I'm hoping that I haven't shared anything "crazy" yet! But, just to make sure we're on the same page, let me explain Jesus' burial:

Afterward Joseph of Arimathea, who had been a secret disciple of Jesus (because he feared the Jewish leaders), asked Pilate for permission to take down Jesus' body. When Pilate gave permission, Joseph came and took the body away. With him came Nicodemus, the man who had come to Jesus at night. He brought about seventy-five pounds of perfumed ointment made from myrrh and aloes. Following Jewish burial custom, they wrapped Jesus' body with the spices in long sheets of linen cloth. The place of crucifixion was near a garden, where there was a new tomb, never used before. And so, because it was the day of preparation for the Jewish Passover and since the tomb was close at hand, they laid Jesus there. - John 19:38-42 (NLT)

These two men, Joseph of Arimathea and Nicodemus (see John chapter 3), are both well-known leaders in Jerusalem; and it was risky for them to go and get the body of Jesus from Pilate. One quirky thing is that Pilate may have given them the body willingly because: (a) these were two respected members of Jewish society, and (b) Pilate had tried to set Jesus free.

When Joseph and Nicodemus get the body, they wrap it in a long sheet coated in spices – including myrrh, the spice we mentioned back at Jesus' birth – and put the body into Joseph's tomb. The amount of spices used was typical for what you would see if you were burying a king. That'll give you an idea of what these men thought about Jesus!

Next, let's talk about the tomb, itself:

Joseph took the body and wrapped it in a long sheet of clean linen cloth. He placed it in his own new tomb, which had been carved out of the rock. Then

he rolled a great stone across the entrance and left. -
Matthew 27:59-60 (NLT)

To bury someone at this time, you placed them on a shelf inside the tomb. After their body decayed, you took their bones – which was all that was left of them – and put them in a bone box called an "ossuary".

But the key here is the stone that's rolled down. You see, outside the tomb, is a small ramp. You push a large stone up that ramp and block it with a smaller stone. When the burial is complete, one person knocks away the small stone, the boulder rolls down to cover the entrance of the tomb, and a V-shaped track locks it in place. To reopen the tomb, you need a lot of men to push the large stone back up the hill!

Next, the religious leaders plan something:

The next day, on the Sabbath, the leading priests and Pharisees went to see Pilate. They told him, "Sir, we remember what that deceiver once said while he was still alive: 'After three days I will rise from the dead.' So we request that you seal the tomb until the third day. This will prevent his disciples from coming and stealing his body and then telling everyone he was raised from the dead! If that happens, we'll be worse off than we were at first."

Pilate replied, "Take guards and secure it the best you can." So they sealed the tomb and posted guards to protect it. - Matthew 27:62-66 (NLT)

Now there IS some debate as to which guard this is and what seal is used.

If the seal and guards came from the religious leaders, they would be well-trained and effective fighters. Also, if you broke the seal, you would be punished by being kicked out of the Temple. In other words, you basically couldn't live in the Land of Israel anymore!

Of course, that's assuming you survived your fight with the guards…

If the seal and guards came from the Romans, then these would be Roman soldiers. These fighters were trained to hold six square feet of ground against an army…and win!

Also, if you broke the seal of Rome, then you would face torture and execution – probably crucifixion – when you were caught. Oh, and there really was nowhere to run to get away from the Roman Empire! (Based on my studies, I do think it was a Roman seal and Roman guards.)

In either case, though, the odds of surviving the battle with the soldiers would require…a miracle!

A Roman Soldier with shield and gladius (sword).

Finally, and this is a really small detail, but it's VERY important:

> *Both Mary Magdalene and the other Mary were sitting across from the tomb and watching. - Matthew 27:61 (NLT)*

So, who all knows where this tomb is? Joseph of Arimathea and Nicodemus – they put the body in the tomb; the religious leaders – they sent guards to seal the tomb; the guards – they're guarding the tomb; and some of the women who followed Jesus – they're watching the tomb be sealed!

Why does any of this matter? It's very important because of what happens next!

Do you remember when I talked about "miracles", and I told you there was one more impossible one to come?

Well, let's take a look at that miracle now!

(9) THE RESURRECTION

We've covered a LOT of ground to get here! Why did we have to talk about all of that other stuff? Well, it's because I want you to know what has happened – from the prophets writing about Jesus' coming before He was born, all the way up through His death and burial – before we get to this final part!

I'm hoping that all of this has made sense so far, because the final miracle that Jesus does is simply incredible! Remember when I told you that *"Extraordinary claims require extraordinary evidence"*? Well, I think this miracle is exactly the extraordinary evidence required to prove that Jesus is the Son of God!

Let me show you what I mean:

Early on Sunday morning, as the new day was dawning, Mary Magdalene and the other Mary went out to visit the tomb.

Suddenly there was a great earthquake! For an angel of the Lord came down from heaven, rolled aside the stone, and sat on it. His face shone like lightning, and his clothing was as white as snow. The guards shook with fear when they saw him, and they fell into a dead faint.

Then the angel spoke to the women. "Don't be afraid!" he said. "I know you are looking for Jesus, who was crucified. He isn't here! He is risen from the dead, just as he said would happen. Come, see where his body was lying. And now, go quickly and tell his disciples that he has risen from the dead, and he is going ahead of you to Galilee. You will see him there. Remember what I have told you."

The women ran quickly from the tomb. They were very frightened but also filled with great joy, and they rushed to give the disciples the angel's message. And as they went, Jesus met them and greeted them. And they ran to him, grasped his feet, and worshiped him. Then Jesus said to them, "Don't be afraid! Go tell my brothers to leave for Galilee, and they will see me there." - Matthew 28:1-10 (NLT)

What happened? Jesus rose from the dead! This same Jesus, born in the little, backwater town of Bethlehem, who grew up as a carpenter, who taught people about God, who performed miracles to prove that He was the Son of God, and who died horribly...came back to life!

An empty tomb in Israel.

Okay, show of hands, how many of you are having trouble believing that? (Not that I can actually see if you've raised your hand!) But if you did, you're not alone:

> *Then the two from Emmaus told their story of how Jesus had appeared to them as they were walking along the road, and how they had recognized him as he was breaking the bread. And just as they were telling about it, Jesus himself was suddenly standing there among them. "Peace be with you," he said. But the whole group was startled and*

frightened, thinking they were seeing a ghost!

"Why are you frightened?" he asked. "Why are your hearts filled with doubt? Look at my hands. Look at my feet. You can see that it's really me. Touch me and make sure that I am not a ghost, because ghosts don't have bodies, as you see that I do." As he spoke, he showed them his hands and his feet.

Still they stood there in disbelief, filled with joy and wonder. Then he asked them, "Do you have anything here to eat?" They gave him a piece of broiled fish, and he ate it as they watched. - Luke 24:35-43 (NLT)

Jesus appears to His Disciples – minus Judas, the guy who betrayed Him – and what's their response? They're terrified because they think Jesus is a ghost! When Jesus tells them to touch His hands, they still think they're seeing a ghost! Finally, Jesus eats some food – the Jews didn't believe that ghosts could eat – and that convinces His followers!

Well, not all of them…

One of the twelve disciples, Thomas (nicknamed the Twin), was not with the others when Jesus came. They told him, "We have seen the Lord!"

But he replied, "I won't believe it unless I see the nail wounds in his hands, put my fingers into them, and place my hand into the wound in his side."

Eight days later the disciples were together again, and this time Thomas was with them. The doors were locked; but suddenly, as before, Jesus was standing among them. "Peace be with you," he said. Then he said to Thomas, "Put your finger here, and look at my hands. Put your hand into the wound in my side. Don't be faithless any longer. Believe!"

"My Lord and my God!" Thomas exclaimed.

Then Jesus told him, "You believe because you have seen me. Blessed are those who believe without seeing me." - John 20:24-29 (NLT)

Now some people have worked very hard to come up with ways to explain all of this away. These ideas include:

The Disciples Stole The Body

I love it when people ask me about this one. The Disciples are **hiding** after Jesus is killed. They thought Jesus was the Messiah, the Savior; but they didn't understand the idea that the Messiah had to die...even though Jesus had told them multiple times!

So, this group of fishermen, tax collectors, and others would have to arm themselves, fight the Romans, move the stone, and steal the body. (None of which is likely to happen!) Then, these Disciples would have to go around and lie to everyone by saying, "We saw Jesus rise from the dead! He's alive!"

Eventually, these men would all be killed – except John – for that lie!

Who would do that?

Legendary Development
In other words, someone, years later, decided to make the story of Jesus more "colorful" and so they added the story of Him rising from the dead.

The problem is that we have writings from just a few years after Jesus was crucified that show the early church believed that Jesus had risen from the dead! There just simply isn't enough time for "legends".

Mass Hallucination
Others argue that the Disciples imagined they saw Jesus because they **wanted** to see Jesus! The problem with this idea is simple, and I can explain it with an example:

Right now, I'm imagining…chocolate! And not just *any* chocolate, I'm imagining my favorite candy bar! Can you also see it? No. Can you imagine what it tastes like? No. Can you imagine eating it? No.

So, just because I can imagine something, it doesn't mean that you can experience it, too! Also, *imagining* a chocolate bar, while nice, still isn't the same as actually *eating* a chocolate bar. (Trust me, I'm hungry now!)

So this idea doesn't work!

Swoon Theory
Some people argue that Jesus wasn't dead and just woke up on His own.

To do that, He would have to get out of the winding sheet – speaking as someone who's studied escapes and escape artists, this isn't easy! – He would have to roll a massive boulder uphill, overpower the guards, and get away.

Then, He would have to show up in a locked room and try to convince His Disciples that He "rose in power"…despite being covered in scabs, scars, and being crippled by the nails.

I don't know about you, but if a guy that

horribly mangled came into my house, I'd start running away! He wouldn't be someone I would worship; He would be a terrifying monster! But that's not the Jesus the Disciples see…

Wrong Tomb
The final theory I want to point out is called "the wrong tomb". In this story, Jesus' followers simply went to the wrong tomb. Because they found the tomb empty, they thought Jesus had risen from the dead!

While this works…somewhat; it really doesn't make much sense.

First of all, like we talked about in the last chapter, there were too many people who knew where the real tomb was! Second, the religious leaders would have produced a body and that would have been the end of the conversation. So this one is unlikely, too!

And speaking of the religious leaders, there *is* another group who becomes convinced that Jesus walked out of the tomb:

As the women were on their way, some of the guards went into the city and told the leading priests what had happened. A meeting with the elders was called, and they decided to give the soldiers a large bribe. They told the soldiers, "You must say, 'Jesus' disciples came during the night while we were sleeping, and they stole his body.' If the governor hears about it, we'll stand up for you so you won't get in trouble." So the guards accepted the bribe and said what they were told to say. Their story spread widely among the Jews, and they still tell it today. - Matthew 28:11-15 (NLT)

In other words, the religious leaders **knew** that Jesus rose from the dead...and lied to cover it up! Why? Because even though Jesus came back, He still wasn't the God that they wanted to follow!

Kind of sad, right?

(10) THE CHOICE

All right, here's where we bring this all in. I've tried to show you that Jesus was a real person, who lived and taught in a real place, at a real time. I've tried to show you that His followers, the Disciples, believed that Jesus was the Son of God because of what they said about Him!

But now the question is: What about you? Who do you believe Jesus is?

- Is He a fictional (fake) storybook character like some people claim?

- Was He just another "good teacher", like others say?

- Was He a liar who tricked a lot of people

into following Him, like some accuse Him of being?

- Or, was Jesus...something else?

Based on everything that I've read, all that I've studied, and all of the people I've talked to, I believe that Jesus really is the Son of God! Even more than that, I believe that Jesus is alive right now, in Heaven, and He wants all of us – you and me! – to believe in Him so that we can come to live with Him someday!

In John 3:16, one of the most famous verses in the whole Bible, Jesus is talking to Nicodemus. (Yep, the guy who came to get Jesus' body!) In the middle of this talk we're told:

"For this is how God loved the world: He gave his one and only Son, so that everyone who believes in him will not perish but have eternal life." - John 3:16 (NLT)

Jesus says to Nicodemus three main things here:

- First of all, Jesus tells us – all of us! – that God loves us! God loves me and God loves you! Now I don't know about your past, but for me, it was hard to believe that anyone could love me. Imagine how I felt when I realized that there IS a God and that God loves me!

- Second, Jesus tells us how important we are to God! We matter so much to Him, that He sent His Son! Jesus lived a perfect life; He didn't have to die. But Jesus, as the "Lamb of God who takes away the sins of the world", died for our mistakes, not His! He was the Passover Lamb, the one who took our punishment, the one who sets us free from our sin, and the one who gives us the ability to live forever in Heaven with Him! That's why Jesus died; it was to take our place!

- Finally, we're told that we can be saved by believing in Jesus! That's it! People try to earn their way to Heaven by proving to God that they can do good things. But Jesus says it isn't about what we do, it's about what God did for us through Him!

Then, if we keep reading in John 3:17, we find:

"God sent his Son into the world not to judge the world, but to save the world through him." - John 3:17 (NLT)

I know a lot of people who think that God hates us and is waiting to punish us for our mistakes! But what does Jesus, the Son of God, say? He says that God doesn't hate us; instead, He wants to save us from our sins! Oh, and that comment about saving "the world"? That includes **you**, too!

Finally, Jesus says in verse 18:

> *"There is no judgment against anyone who believes in him. But anyone who does not believe in him has already been judged for not believing in God's one and only Son." - John 3:18 (NLT)*

Get this! It all comes down to a choice!

You can choose to read a book like this, examine what it says, and then decide you're *not* going to follow Jesus! God gives you the choice to walk away from Him; just like God gave humans the choice to sin way back in the beginning!

And, if you choose to not follow Jesus, then you can't be surprised when God looks at you and says, "Go away from Me! I never knew you!" This also means that Heaven is not your final home!

It's your choice...

On the other hand, you can choose to read a book like this, examine what it says, and decide that Jesus really is the Son of God! If you realize that you've sinned by breaking God's laws, that you can't save yourself from the punishment of sin (none of us are good enough to do that on our own); if you believe in Jesus with your whole heart; and if you give your life to Him, then Jesus has promised that you **will** be saved.

This means that one day, in Heaven, God will look at you and say, "Welcome home, My child!"

If you're reading this and you want to ask Jesus to be your Savior, to put Him in charge of your life, then you simply need to talk to Him. There are no magical words, no special phrases! All it takes is a simple, honest conversation.

To do that today, you can pray something like this:

> *Dear God. I know that I've made mistakes, what the Bible calls "sins". I've done bad things. Please forgive me for my mistakes. Please come into my life. Please save me! From now on, help me to put you in charge of my life. Help me to follow You. With the faith I have, I choose you today. Thank you for loving me. In Jesus' name I pray. Amen.*

If you prayed that prayer and meant it, I look forward to seeing you in Heaven someday!

CONTINUING YOUR JOURNEY

If you've decided to follow Jesus, then I have some suggestions for you as you get started. (Even if you don't believe in Jesus, some of these steps are for you, too!)

<u>Read The Bible</u>
If you're new to the Bible, I would like to recommend that you start in the Book of John in the New Testament. That's "John", not "1 John", "2 John", or "3 John". (John wrote a few different books!)

John is a man who followed Jesus, heard Him teach, saw Him do miracles, and then he wrote about everything in an easy-to-understand way.

One word of warning: John gets *very* excited about Jesus in John chapter one and uses some

HUGE words and ideas to describe Him! After that, John calms down and tells you what you need to know about Jesus in simple, basic words. If you get lost in chapter one, skip to chapter two and you'll be all set!

Pray
Prayer is simply talking to God, just like you would talk to anyone else. You don't have to kneel, sit, stand, or lay down! You don't have to lift your hands, fold them, or keep them to your side. You can pray with your eyes opened or closed. Finally, there are no fancy words that you need to say.

When I pray, I end up just talking to God. I ask Him to help me with my problems, to trust Him when things aren't going well, and to thank Him for all He's doing in my life!

Believe God's Word, Not Your Feelings
When I became a Christian, the man who told me about Jesus – Hi Ira! – gave me a small book. In it I read, "The first thing that Satan will try to do is tell you, 'You're not saved!'"

Satan is our enemy; he stands against God. And Satan uses our feelings to try to convince us that God hates us, God can't forgive us, or that we really aren't following God anyhow! I've had many times when I didn't "feel" saved; even though I **knew** I was saved!

So, if your feelings are telling you the wrong thing, what do you do? If you "feel" like you're separated from God, I recommend that you go and check out Romans 8:35 and 37:

> *Can anything ever separate us from Christ's love? Does it mean he no longer loves us if we have trouble or calamity, or are persecuted, or hungry, or destitute, or in danger, or threatened with death? … No, despite all these things, overwhelming victory is ours through Christ, who loved us. - Romans 8:35 and 37 (NLT)*

If you're having a really down day, go read all of Romans 8! It's what I do when I need some encouragement in my life!

Hang Out With Other Christians

You can start going to church on Sunday mornings, you can join a Bible Study at your church or school, or you can even find a "Small Group" which gives you a bunch of Christian friends to hang out with and learn from. By surrounding yourself with others who believe in Jesus, you can grow in your own faith, too!

My only word of caution is to find a church

that believes in the Bible. If they say, "The Bible says this, but we believe that!" they probably can't tell you much about Jesus!

Unfortunately, there are a lot of churches out there who no longer believe in the Bible. Instead, they teach whatever they want to or what makes them "feel" good. (Remember my warning about *not* relying on your feelings?)

After becoming a Christian, I went to a small-town church with an excellent Pastor who made sure I spent time in prayer and reading the Bible! (I became a Pastor, in part, because of his example!)

Get Some "Good" Books

I love to not only read what God says in His Word, the Bible; I also like to read what other people think about God!

If you go to a bookstore, this type of book can be VERY expensive. If you go to your local church, a lot of them will lend these books to you free-of-charge! (I also like to shop at used book stores for these, too!)

My library has grown to over 2,000 books about God, Jesus, Israel, and more! (My wife hates it when we have to move!)

Final Thoughts:

In the end, know that you're not alone in this journey! If you're a Christian, not only has Jesus saved you, not only is God going with you, not only is the Holy Spirit living inside of you – that's another topic for another time – but know that I am praying for you, wherever you are!

May God bless you on the adventures you go through with Him!

ABOUT THE AUTHOR

My name is Barry Rudesill and I am a pastor, teacher, author, and speaker. I've spent over 30 years in full-time ministry, working with churches, camps, schools, and many individuals and families, too! My goal is simply to serve when and how I can.

When I'm not writing books, I'm teaching a program called *"The Trek"* that helps people to discover who God is and who they are because of Him! Feel free to check out *The Trek* at www.thetrek.org.

Other than that, I live with my wife, Maria; my two children, Isaac and Lauren; and three hounds who like to sleep at my feet while I write!